I Can Divide,
I Need No Guide!

Tracy Kompelien

Consulting Editors, Diane Craig, M.A./Reading Specialist
and Susan Kosel, M.A. Education

ABDO
Publishing Company

Published by ABDO Publishing Company, 4940 Viking Drive, Edina, Minnesota 55435.

Printed in the United States.

Credits
Edited by: Pam Price
Curriculum Coordinator: Nancy Tuminelly
Cover and Interior Design and Production: Mighty Media
Photo Credits: ShutterStock, Wewerka Photography

Library of Congress Cataloging-in-Publication Data

Kompelien, Tracy, 1975-
  I can divide, I need no guide! / Tracy Kompelien
    p. cm. -- (Math made fun)
  ISBN 10 1-59928-515-0 (hardcover)
  ISBN 10 1-59928-516-9 (paperback)

  ISBN 13 978-1-59928-515-3 (hardcover)
  ISBN 13 978-1-59928-516-0 (paperback)
  1. Division--Juvenile literature. I. Title. II. Series.

QA115.K663 2007
513.2'14--dc22
                                                    2006015296

SandCastle Level: Transitional

SandCastle™ books are created by a professional team of educators, reading specialists, and content developers around five essential components—phonemic awareness, phonics, vocabulary, text comprehension, and fluency—to assist young readers as they develop reading skills and strategies and increase their general knowledge. All books are written, reviewed, and leveled for guided reading, early reading intervention, and Accelerated Reader® programs for use in shared, guided, and independent reading and writing activities to support a balanced approach to literacy instruction. The SandCastle™ series has four levels that correspond to early literacy development. The levels help teachers and parents select appropriate books for young readers.

Emerging Readers
(no flags)

Beginning Readers
(1 flag)

Transitional Readers
(2 flags)

Fluent Readers
(3 flags)

These levels are meant only as a guide. All levels are subject to change.

I can divide

by separating things into two or more equal groups or parts.

Words used to talk about division:

equal
groups
number sentence
parts
quotient
share

$$4 \div 2 = 2$$

divided by   equals   quotient

Here are two ways to write the number sentence for 4 divided by 2 equals 2. The answer to a division problem is called the quotient.

4

÷ 2

2

These and these are equal groups.

The 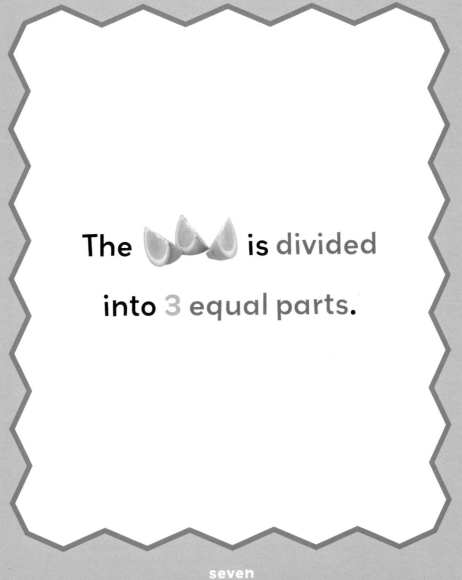 is divided into 3 equal parts.

This group of

is equal to

this group of .

There are
2 groups of
3 pencils.

The are divided into 4 equal groups.

I Can Divide, I Need No Guide!

Clyde has some peas that he wants to share with Louise.

I am starting with a total of 8 peas.

twelve

12

"I think," says Clyde, "that if I divide, we can each have a share. That will be fair."

I have divided the peas into 2 equal groups.

fourteen
14

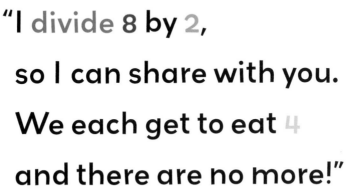

"I divide 8 by 2,

so I can share with you.

We each get to eat 4

and there are no more!"

8 divided by 2
equals 4.

Dividing
Every Day!

There are 10 cards in all.
I have divided the cards
into 2 groups of 5.

$10 \div 2 = 5$

I divide my muffin into 2 equal parts.

I have 24 eggs. If I put 4 eggs in each bowl, I will need 6 bowls.

$24 \div 4 = 6$

twenty-two

22

How can you equally share 6 cookies between 2 people?

$6 \div 2 = 3$ cookies each!

Glossary

divide – to separate into equal groups or parts.

equal – having exactly the same amount. Equal groups have the same amount in each group.

number sentence – a math problem in which the numbers on each side of the equal sign name the same amount.

quotient – the answer to a division problem.